Hickory Flat Public Library
2740 East Cherokee Drive
Canton, Georgia 30115

Everglades National Park

Bobbie Kalman

🌳 Crabtree Publishing Company

www.crabtreebooks.com

Created by Bobbie Kalman

For Chris Jackson,

with much thanks for all the help you have given us

Author and Editor-in-Chief
Bobbie Kalman

Research
Enlynne Paterson

Editors
Kathy Middleton
Enlynne Paterson

Proofreader
Crystal Sikkens

Photo research
Bobbie Kalman

Design
Bobbie Kalman
Katherine Berti
Samantha Crabtree (cover)

Production coordinator
Katherine Berti

Illustrations
Katherine Berti: page 4
Bonna Rouse: page 14
Margaret Amy Salter: page 16

Photographs
BigStockPhoto: page 24 (bottom left and right)
iStockphoto: page 30
Lauren Kinsey/sweetmagnoliaphoto.com: page 28
Shutterstock: cover, pages 1, 3, 5, 6, 7, 8, 9, 10, 11, 12,
   13, 15, 16, 17, 18, 19, 20, 21, 22, 23, 24 (middle right),
   25, 26, 27, 29
Wikimedia Commons: Lori Oberhofer, National Park
   Service: page 31
Other images by Corel

Library and Archives Canada Cataloguing in Publication

Kalman, Bobbie, 1947-
   Everglades National Park / Bobbie Kalman.

(Introducing habitats)
Includes index.
ISBN 978-0-7787-2960-0 (bound).--ISBN 978-0-7787-2988-4 (pbk.)

   1. Wetland ecology--Florida--Everglades National Park--Juvenile
literature. 2. Natural history--Florida--Everglades National
Park--Juvenile literature. I. Title. II. Series: Introducing habitats

QH105.F6K34 2010   j577.09759'39   C2009-903644-4

Library of Congress Cataloging-in-Publication Data

Kalman, Bobbie.
   Everglades National Park / Bobbie Kalman.
      p. cm. -- (Introducing habitats)
   Includes index.
   ISBN 978-0-7787-2988-4 (pbk. : alk. paper) -- ISBN 978-0-7787-2960-0
(reinforced library binding · alk. paper)
   1. Natural history--Florida--Everglades National Park--Juvenile literature.
   2. Wetland ecology--Florida--Everglades National Park--Juvenile literature.
   I. Title. II. Series.

QH105.F6K35 2010
508.759'39--dc22

2009023336

Crabtree Publishing Company

www.crabtreebooks.com   1-800-387-7650

Published in Canada
Crabtree Publishing
616 Welland Ave.
St. Catharines, ON
L2M 5V6

Published in the United States
Crabtree Publishing
PMB16A
350 Fifth Ave., Suite 3308
New York, NY 10118

Published in the United Kingdom
Crabtree Publishing
Maritime House
Basin Road North, Hove
BN41 1WR

Published in Australia
Crabtree Publishing
386 Mt. Alexander Rd.
Ascot Vale (Melbourne)
VIC 3032

Contents

What is a national park?

Everglades is a huge **national park** in southeast Florida. A national park is an area of land that is protected by a government so plants and animals can live there safely. People are not allowed to build or hunt in national parks. They are not allowed to hurt the plants or animals that live in them. Everglades National Park is about 100 miles (160 km) long and 50 miles (80 km) wide. Most of it is covered with water.

PENSACOLA

TALLAHASSEE

JACKSONVILLE

FLORIDA

DAYTONA BEACH

ORLANDO

TAMPA

CAPE CORAL

FORT LAUDERDALE

MIAMI

EVERGLADES NATIONAL PARK

KEY LARGO

KEY WEST

What are habitats?

Everglades National Park is a large area that is made up of different kinds of **habitats**. Habitats are the natural homes of plants and animals. There are **living things** in habitats. Plants and animals are living things. There are also **non-living things** in habitats. Sunshine, air, rocks, soil, and water are non-living things. An **ecosystem** forms when living things work together with the non-living parts of their habitats. Water is a very big part of the Everglades ecosystem.

plants

rock

alligators

water

Name two living things in this picture. Name two non-living things that you can see. Name two non-living things that you cannot see.

5

Everglades wetlands

The Everglades is made up mainly of **wetlands**. A wetland is land that is covered with water. Some wetlands are under water all year. Other wetlands are covered with water for only part of the year. The Everglades has two main kinds of wetlands. They are **swamps** and **marshes**. Swamps are wetlands with trees. The picture below shows a swamp.

Marshes have no trees

Marshes are shallow, grassy wetlands without trees. About three-quarters of the Everglades is **sawgrass marsh**. Sawgrass marsh is a slow-moving river in which sawgrass grows. Sawgrass is not really grass. It is a sedge. The roots of sedges can get flooded, but the plants do not drown. The edges of sawgrass leaves look like the teeth on a saw blade. That is why the plant is called sawgrass.

This great egret is looking for food in a sawgrass marsh.

Everglades at a glance

Most of the Everglades is covered with shallow, moving water. It also has areas of deeper water and dry land. **Sloughs** look like small rivers that are about three feet (1 m) deeper than the water in the marshes around them. Birds, alligators, turtles, ducks, and many other animals find water and food in sloughs.

sawgrass marsh

slough

8

Islands of trees

Land areas that are a little higher than marshes are called **hardwood hammocks**. Many kinds of trees grow in hammocks. Hammocks are also home to animals that live on land (see pages 24–25). Pinelands are even higher than hammocks. They are dry habitats in the eastern part of the Everglades. The Florida panther (see page 28) lives in the pinelands. The pinelands are also home to many snakes.

hardwood hammock

slough

9

Everglades weather

The Everglades is the largest **subtropical wilderness** in the United States. It has a summer **wet season** and a winter **dry season**. The wet season lasts from June to November. This summer season is very hot, and it rains nearly every day. The park is almost completely covered in water during this time. In winter, large parts of the Everglades dry up. Only the deeper areas stay wet. Animals crowd into the deeper places to find water.

The Everglades is green in the wet season and brown in the dry season. Which season is this?

During the dry season, there is very little water in the marshes and swamps, so the plants dry out.

Fire!

Fire is a natural part of life in the Everglades. Fires are started by lightning during the dry season. Some trees need the heat of fire to help spread their seeds. Fires also help clear out dead plants and plants that do not belong in the Everglades. Sawgrass can survive fires because its roots are under water.

Everglades water

Most of the water in the wetlands of the Everglades is **fresh water**. Fresh water has very little salt. Oceans have **salt water**. Salt water has a lot of salt in it. Where the Everglades meets the ocean, the water is **brackish**. Brackish water is a mixture of salt water and fresh water.

These birds find fish and other animals to eat in this brackish water.

"Gator" holes

Alligators need plenty of water, but during the dry winter months, there may not be enough water for these big animals. To stay alive, alligators dig **gator holes**. Gator holes fill with water, and they also bring food to the alligators. Fish, snakes, turtles, lizards, frogs, birds, and insects move in with the alligators until it starts raining again. How would you like to spend your winter in a gator hole?

This egret finds food and water at a gator hole. Will it become food for a gator?

13

Food energy

All living things need **energy**.
Energy is the power to grow, move,
and stay alive. Energy comes from
sunlight. Plants use air, water, and
the energy in sunlight to make
food. Using sunlight to make
food is called **photosynthesis**.

sun

*A plant's
leaves take
in sunlight
and air.*

*A plant gets water
through its roots.*

14

Grasses use sunlight to make food.

What is a food chain?

Plants use the sun's energy to make food, but animals cannot make their own food. They get energy by eating other living things. When one living thing eats another living thing, there is a **food chain**. The Everglades ecosystem has many food chains.

*Rabbits eat grasses. They are **herbivores**. Herbivores are animals that eat plants.*

*Alligators and crocodiles eat rabbits. They are **carnivores**. Carnivores are animals that eat other animals.*

Water plants

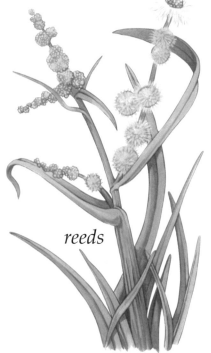

reeds

Plants start food chains, but only certain plants can grow in soggy wetland soil. Sawgrass, reeds, and cattails grow in marshes, where the water is shallow. **Algae** covers water like a mat. Algae is like a plant, but it has no roots. Many animals feed on algae.

cattail

swamp lily

reeds

This picture shows some plants that grow in marshes. They are reeds, swamp lilies, and algae.

algae

16

Growing in water

Water lilies called spatterdock grow in the deeper waters of the sloughs. They have large green leaves that float on top of the water. The leaves take in sunlight and air. The roots of the spatterdock plants are under water.

spatterdock

sawgrass

17

Trees in water

Very few trees can grow in wetlands, but cypress trees and mangroves can. These trees are specially **adapted**, or suited, to their wet habitats. Cypress trees can grow on land or in water. Their thick **knees**, or bases, hold the trees steady when water flows around them.

knees

Mangrove swamps

Parts of the Everglades are beside the ocean. Here, fresh water mixes with salty ocean water. Mangrove trees grow in this brackish water. The roots of mangroves hold the trees high above water. They keep soil from being washed away during storms. Animals live in the roots, as well as at the tops, of mangroves. This hawk has built a nest at the top of this mangrove tree.

Animals in water

A crocodile's snout is shaped like the letter V. When the crocodile closes its mouth, its long teeth stick out.

Many animals find food and water in the marshes and swamps of the Everglades. The most famous animal in the Everglades is the American alligator. Crocodiles also live in the Everglades. Southern Florida is the only place where both alligators and crocodiles live side by side, but they do not get along!

An alligator's snout is shaped like the letter U. When the alligator closes its mouth, only a few of its teeth show. The animals on the right are alligators. You can tell by their rounded snouts.

Many kinds of turtles live in swamps and marshes. This turtle is a softshell turtle. Softshell turtles eat fish, snails, insects, and frogs. Their shells are not hard like the shells of most turtles. They are more like leather.

Many kinds of fish also live in the waters of the Everglades. This fish is a catfish.

Frogs and toads live in the waters of the Everglades.

Fish make tasty meals for birds such as this anhinga.

21

Wading birds

Many kinds of **wading birds** can be seen in the Everglades. Wading birds are birds with long legs. They **wade**, or walk slowly through water, to find food. Storks, herons, roseate spoonbills, ibises, flamingos, and egrets are wading birds that live in the Everglades.

Roseate spoonbills sweep their bills from side to side. They look for fish to eat in the water. Spoonbills live in the parts of the Everglades that are near the ocean. (See map on page 4.)

The Everglades is the only place in North America where American flamingos live in nature. They get their red color from eating algae and shrimps.

Great egrets find fish and frogs to eat in water. On land, they feed on mice, insects, and lizards.

Ibises dig into mud for shrimps and small crabs. This ibis is looking for food in a swamp.

The great blue heron is the largest wading bird in the Everglades. It eats the fish and frogs in the water. On land, the heron eats snakes, mice, and lizards. This great blue heron is having a catfish for lunch.

Living on land

Some of the animals that live on land in the Everglades are gray foxes, raccoons, tree frogs, fox squirrels, skunks, opossums, deer, rabbits, and armadillos. These animals live in the hardwood hammock and pineland habitats.

baby gray fox

raccoon

marsh rabbit

pygmy rattlesnake

24

deer

fox squirrel

black bear

striped skunk

All the animals shown on these pages, except one, are **mammals**. Mammals have hair or fur on their bodies. Which animal has no hair or fur? Which is not a mammal?

armadillo

opossum

Answer: pygmy rattlesnake

25

Everglades babies

Animals that live in the Everglades raise their babies there. Baby birds and alligators **hatch**, or break out of eggs. Mammal babies are born. After animal babies hatch or are born, they grow and change until they are adults. As adults, they can make their own babies. Growing from babies to adults is called a **life cycle**.

Opossum babies are mammals that are born. After they are born, their mother carries them around and feeds them milk from her body.

Baby alligators hatch from eggs. Their mother carries them to water soon after the babies hatch.

This great blue heron is feeding one of her **chicks**, or baby birds. The baby sticks its head into the mother's mouth. The mother then brings up food from her stomach. The second chick wants some food, too. It is telling its mother that it is hungry!

27

Endangered animals

Endangered animals are animals that are in danger of becoming **extinct**. Extinct animals are no longer alive in nature or on Earth. Everglades National Park protects several endangered animals from becoming extinct.

*The Florida panther is the most endangered animal in the Everglades. Only 50-100 are still alive! This mother panther lives in the pinelands with her **cub**, or baby cat.*

28

American alligators were once endangered, but now there are more than a million of them in Florida. Many live in the Everglades. There are fewer than 1,000 American crocodiles in Florida, however.

Wood storks may soon become endangered.

Florida manatees are on the endangered list. They live near the ocean in brackish water.

We need wetlands!

Wetlands are very important to the Earth. They clean pollution from water and stop flooding. They provide animals with places to live and raise their young. Birds that **migrate**, or move to warmer places for winter, stop at wetlands for food and water. The Everglades also collects rainfall and provides people in Florida with water. Everglades National Park protects the water supply that is very important to plants, animals, and people!

Visiting Everglades National Park is an amazing experience!

Strangers to the Everglades

Some people have brought animals to the Everglades that do not belong there, such as **exotic** pets. Exotic pets come from faraway places. Most of the animals die when they are trapped or on their way to North America. After people buy the pets that have survived, many find that they cannot look after them. These pet owners then dump the unwanted animals outdoors. Thousands of exotic pets, such as Burmese pythons, parrots, fish, and lizards are being dumped in the Everglades. These animals are not **native** to, or part of the ecosystem of, the Everglades. They change the food chains and cause big problems by eating the foods that the native animals need in order to survive. You can help the Everglades and other habitats by not buying exotic pets. Ask your friends to do the same, and NEVER dump any pet in the wild.

The Burmese python above is one of the thousands of snakes that are now living in the Everglades. An alligator and the snake are fighting.

Glossary

Note: Some boldfaced words are defined where they appear in the book.

brackish Slightly salty water

ecosystem Plants, animals, and other living things working together in their non-living environment

endangered Describing a plant or animal that is in danger of dying out

food chain The pattern of eating and being eaten

habitat The natural home of a plant or animal

hardwood hammock An area of land that is slightly above the water in a marsh

marsh A shallow, grassy wetland with no trees

national park A piece of land where plants and animals live and which is protected by the government

slough Small rivers that are deeper than the water in the marshes around them

subtropical wilderness Describing a warm area of land that is above or below the tropics at the equator

swamp A wetland area in which trees grow

wetland An area of land that is under water some or all of the time

Index

Printed in the U.S.A.—BG